Copyright Information

ISBN 9781703102994

Independently Published

First Edition: October 2019

www.thatdamnlawyer.com

That Damn Lawyer Presents: The Copyright Handbook

By:

Brian H. Hanning

www.thatdamnlawyer.com

Welcome Reader

Reader,

I would love to tell you I started my law firm for some altruistic reason, to save the world. Or, because I grew up knowing I would own my own business one day and after going through law school immediately decided to hang a shingle.

No, the truth is both stranger and simpler. I had an internship right out of law school and when that ended, I found a position as the only associate in a previously one person shop. When I stepped away from the firm, I had a couple of clients wanting to follow me and a new client asking about a project.

Of course, without knowing how to run a business, I agreed. Soon, I had my company formed, with a bank account and everything, and was out trying to drum up additional business. That was June.

It wasn't until December that I took the time to slow down and really delve into a business plan.

Running a business is complicated and it can be incredibly rewarding. You get to be the boss, the salesman, the person doing the actual work of the business, and everything in between. I, in all honesty, love it. I can also see how all this legal stuff can be daunting.

That is why I wrote this Handbook, and others, to help people in similar situations answer some of those legal questions. Law ends up being behind the scenes in so many ways in our lives. Whether we are out making a documentary or installing windows, driving packages or creating marketing.

Each topic I cover is something relevant to one kind of business or another, be it a hobby turned side gig such as a photo challenge or a passion project turned day job or any other situation where you become your own boss.

Which may raise the question of why listen to me?

The answer being, this is what I do in my day job. I help small businesses understand law. I get to help people understand why some document or concept is needed. Every day at my law firm, I help businesses in one way or another.

I know many people start their business on the smallest of budgets. Searching for answers or guidance to fit your business can be daunting. I highly suggest getting in contract with your local resources, such as: the Small Business Development Centers, business and non-profit resource librarians, or pro bono centers such as the Attorneys for the Arts programs. It is in making connections and meeting the right resources which can help you be successful in all of your goals.

And so, Reader, welcome to this Handbook.

I will say that once you read this and if it is something that resonates with you, please keep it close to hand. Sometimes, being able to double check can help keep things clear for you.

Best of luck with your endeavors!

Brian H. Hanning

www.thatdamnlawyer.com

Table of Contents

Introduction

Human creativity has generated amazing art which informs, shapes, and maintains our culture and creative expression. This includes our movies, books, music, podcasts, and so much more as new forms of creativity continue to evolve. These are just a few examples that are part of daily life.

The importance of art and creativity, and its impact on human development and culture both from a personal fulfillment and historical perspective, demand we use clear legal tools to protect it and the creator. One tool that helps put reasonably clear, specific guidelines in place is Copyright law. These laws promote the prevalence of art in ways we love and enjoy regularly, while ensuring the creators are recognized and their ownership of what they create is protected.

It's important to remember art can be individual, but it also can be collaborative. This leads to slightly different protections under Copyright law. We will review substantial protections offered by Copyright Law in this Handbook to provide you with a core understanding of how the protections could work for you and potential steps to take in relation to the type of creation you make.

Depending on your goals with your art and self expression, there is a lot you can chose to do with your art, including selling, teaching, curating, freely sharing, and more. It's not often you outwardly express those creative goals and intentions to the wider world when creating. Copyright law, at its core, helps you think about, outline, as well as legally define and protect your creative works, and is extremely useful in reaching your creative goals. Whether your art is for work or a hobby, Copyright law is a powerful tool, while allowing you to focus on the artistic expression and have fun.

industry related peers. Resources including mentors and public resources in your community can be extremely valuable in shaping and growing your creative ideas and talents.

This Handbook outlines what you need to know as a creator, how you can protect your ideas, work and time, and ways to think about your artistic work from a personal, business, and legal standpoint, along with the tools you may need depending on the creative goals you want to reach.

Section A: Disclosures

As a lawyer, I support and educate people about legal issues and concerns for their business and hobbies, including how decisions can affect their rights. The majority of this Handbook provides expert advice to help you understand the basics of Copyright, including what is protected and the extent of that protection.

This Handbook covers the **specifics of Copyright law in the United States** and some common examples that often arise for creators. This Handbook does not cover the Copyright Directive of the European Union or other laws. The resources and comments provided here are provided for guidance and general assistance. Some law is quoted and any interpretations of the law are generalizations, not legal advice and you need to contact an attorney to discuss the specifics of your case.

To the extent law is quoted, it is from **Title 17 of the United States Code**. The quotes are for guidance and reference. Case law has interpreted these statutes, which can vastly change their meaning from what is presented depending on a number of factors. Do not assume the laws as presented in this Handbook apply to your specific situation.

No attorney client relationship is formed by the basis of referring to this book. If legal assistance is needed, it is best for you to contact an attorney with expertise and experience in Copyright. To the extent a question arises about your particular situation, hire a Copyright attorney and describe the full context to them.

Section B: A Note on Capitalizations

You may notice through this Handbook strange capitalizations or bolds. For example, "Copyright" and "**Title 17.**" These exist for two reasons.

First, I recognize language can be tricky. After all, copyright can refer to the artistic or creative works with legal rights related to them. And Copyright is the legal shorthand for the body of laws required by the United States Constitution to protect certain works.

As such, I will attempt to provide clarity by how I refer to the concepts. There is "Copyright" which refers broadly to the idea of a body of laws, including statutes and cases, which explain the protections and limitations on art and creative works. On the other hand, there are the copyrights, the specific rights discussed in this Handbook or the status of having a copyright. By capitalizing one and occasionally providing further context, I am trying to distinguish related concepts with separate definitions created by the system.

I will bold **Title 17** and various statutory provisions as it is the important source.

Article 1: What is Copyright?

Copyright is the name given to the body of law designed to protect 'artistic' work. In this case, artistic means any work that has some artistic creativity and creative thought involved in making the work.

Importantly, an 'artistic work' with 'artistic creativity' is not a reference to the veracity or quality of the work. Non-fiction, such as landscape paintings or photographs, memoirs, and the like are not disqualified because they are 'non-fiction.' We will get into the standard later.

For our purposes, an 'artistic work' is something creative, to some degree. A creative work may or may not use and combine existing elements to present something original.

Now, Copyright law defines:

- what kind of works are protected,

- what the rights in the protection are,

- when there is a violation of those rights,

- what some defenses are,

And more.

As people, we like to push boundaries. The authors of copyright protected works are no different. Technology has enhanced the ability of authors to create a wider array of works at home or with more ease than before. As such, Copyright can have quirks attributable to the speed of changing law versus the speed of technology in a practical setting.

If you are an author under Copyright law, registering your work can be one of the best investments you ever make.

Section A: Sources of Copyright Law

In the United States Constitution, Congress is explicitly given the power to:

"promote the progress of science and useful arts, by securing for limited times to authors and inventors the exclusive right to their respective writings and discoveries."

Article I Section 8 Clause 8.

This clause is the source of all Copyright law in the United States.

Congress created a series of laws, amended fairly frequently, to describe and establish what is Copyright. Those laws are all located in **Title 17** of the United States Code.

We will be referring to these statues frequently in this Handbook. In fact, the language of Copyright law plays an important role in defining our understanding of copyrights. This means the law of Copyright is primarily based in statute, with explanations or expansions in case law, meaning courts have determined outcomes of cases which are used as precedent and guidance by lawyers.

So the law is there technically, but what does it mean on a practical level? It means if there is a question about Copyrights generally, the first place to look is **Title 17**. Even if there is no direct answer for your specific question, there is definitely a rule, or rules, to help frame decision making or offer a more precise answer.

Section B: When does a Copyright Exist?

Copyright protection for a work exists when a work is created, or:

> "Copyright protection subsists, in accordance with this title, in original works of authorship fixed in any tangible medium of expression, now known or later

developed, from which they can
be perceived, reproduced, or
otherwise communicated, either
directly or with the aid of a
machine or device." § 102.

Now, let's break this down into something practical
and useful.

- "Copyright protection subsists" - is considered to
  be automatic protection. If a work qualifies, then
  the work has most of the protections of Copyright
  law. There are other steps to ensure all
  protections, but creation is the first and most
  important step obtaining protection under
  Copyright law.

- "original works of authorship fixed in any tangible
  medium of expression" - This test determines
  what works qualify for Copyright protection. It is
  shaped using a variety of defined terms, including

original, work, authorship, and fixed, which are defined in **Title 17**. For our purposes, this aspect stands for the idea that when one or more people create something artistic or creative whatever was created is likely a protected work.

- "in any tangible medium of expression, . . . from which they can be . . . communicated" - Means a third party can experience the work. It does not mean a third party has or will be your audience, only that an audience is possible. The end of the section also works with the concerns about technology, allowing for an experience of a creative to evolve beyond what is currently common or possible. In other words, it does not really matter how it was communicated, instead the focus is on if it can be communicated to an audience.

The main goal, reaching back to the purpose originally addressed Constitution, is the advancement of the arts and sciences. This means this test of protected works has to be understood from that perspective. The perspective that an author (using the jargon of Copyright), you as an individual or a team, created art.

In the big picture, Copyright law is a protection of art, of creativity, of personal expression. These tests for defining art, creativity, and expression must be focused on those concepts and broadly interpreted.

Works which can be protected can be a play or a podcast, a video essay or a musical composition. It can be a biography or the story of a brave group of voyagers traveling the stars. It can be a painting of yourself or a sculpture depicting a story that keeps poking at you to be expressed.

While you can take a photograph and hang it in your basement, it is capable of being seen and appreciated by more than your mind. It is capable of finding an audience. That does not mean it has to be displayed for any and everyone. In this case, Copyright law considers the possibilities of how a creative work may be shown or communicated, not just if it has been communicated or not.

All that matters is an author made something and that something can find its audience.

Subsection 1: Originality
Let's touch on the word "original."

Original *does not* have a definition in **Title 17**. However, that does not mean we are resigned to falling back on to the common sense, colloquial use of the word.

Original means "only that the work was independently created . . . and that it possesses at least some minimal degree of creativity." *Feist Publications v Rural telephone service*, 499 U.S. 340, 345 (1991).

That means if you, the author, or a team of authors, create something that is not a copy of someone else work, it is <u>likely</u> to be original.

This happens all the time. People (2 or more) come up with an idea such as paranormal romance. They use similar tropes such as sexy vampire or the meet-cute. Under Copyright the basic story premise can be similar and as long as the author(s) create their own versions, it will be most likely be considered original.

Think about it - how many lovable rogues exist? Each has their own spin or twist, which makes it original, even if the character is a trope. As Judge Learned Hand wrote "we are rather concerned with the line between expression and what is expressed." *Nichols v. Universal Pictures Corporation*, 45 F.2d 119, 121 (1930).

It is the details that matter and this is why most, but not all, works of "art" will qualify for copyright protection.

Subsection 2: Focus on Expression

By virtue of "original" and the test for qualification, Copyright extends to a great many things. However, Copyright does not extend to everything. Instead, Copyright protection specifically _does not_ include:

"any idea, procedure, process, system, method of operation, concept, principle, or discovery, regardless of the form in which it is described, explained, illustrated, or embodied." **§102(b)**.

In other words, Copyright protects your expression of an idea. It is the details which make art special and unique. Yet, Copyright does not protect ideas, in part because a broad enough idea can be in an enormous number of works.

Here's an example to help make this part of Copyright law clearer:

I, a sculptor, am going to create a sculpture of an idol of mine - Michelangelo. It is going to show him in the best possible light and it will be put in a town square for everyone to wander by and admire. This is my idea, my creative intention.

The expression of that creative intention is when I come with the final sculpture and it is a turtle with a paintbrush. Or a play on the famous artist through the lens of the Teenage Mutant Ninja Turtles character, both of which share a name - Michelangelo.

At the same time, another person can a similar creative intention, and instead create a bust of a young man with a long beard and rolled hat. Yet another person may craft a photorealistic, full body statue of an androgynous person wearing stereotypical renaissance period Italian clothing.

This is Copyright law means by "the idea" - <u>it is the basic pitch</u>. <u>Expression is the result</u>.

Remember, expression can be of more than one idea. In all of these examples, the pitch was for a statue of Michelangelo. However, each person who made the statue brought other creative elements into their interpretation as well.

When it comes to Copyright, the interpretation is the same with essentially every other work. There is more than one idea, which gets distilled into the pitch and to the background. The expression is how those ideas work together as a whole.

Section C: What Types of Works Can Be Copyrighted?

Within the universe of works that can be granted Copyright protection, not all of them probably should receive protection. After all, the Constitutional goal is limited and so is **Title 17**. As such, Copyright law recognizes specific categories of works to be protected.

Protectable works include:

- Literary works;

- Musical works, including any accompanying words;

- Dramatic works, including any accompanying music;

- Pantomimes and choreographic works;

- Pictorial, graphic, and sculptural works;

- Motion pictures and other audiovisual works;

- Sound recordings; and

- Architectural works.

See §102 for the list and §101 for definitions of each category (though the titles do a fairly good job at conveying a broad meaning of the categories).

When creating something, it is common for a work to fall within more than one of the categories. As mentioned, when creating something, it can be desirable to push boundaries.These eight categories are fairly broad, but they are categorical and represent different of types of works.

The nice thing from a creator's perspective is a work may be registered in as many categories as necessary.

For example, think of a video game. Many games have at least some form of storyline, providing motivation to reach the next level and see what happens next. Then there are cutscenes, which may include voice work along with significant animation work. In addition, there are characters and level design, along with the overall design of the user interface. Most games also include some musical, sometimes purely orchestral, other times original songs with lyrics or current top 40 hits that need to be licensed for use.

This game does not fit within one category of works. In fact, it could be argued a "video game" does not fit within any category.

Yet, the work is likely to be protected.

The story is a literary or dramatic work.

The cutscenes are motion pictures. And the audio, the voice work, is a sound recording, if not part of an audiovisual protection.

The character and level designs are series pictorial works.

The music, the score and the songs are both sound recordings, lyrics, and compositions.

Almost every, if not every part, of the game is protected as a whole and separately.

Complex works that cannot be easily categorized end up being split - protected though multiple categories.

Section D: How Long Does Copyright Protection Last?

One slight wording note with the language of the Copyright Act is inherent in the word "author." "Author" is used to represent both the singular and plural. As such, the author can be:

- An individual

- Multiple authors

- Anonymous individuals or teams, and

- Works made on the job

This has a direct impact on how long copyright protection lasts.

Copyright protection lasts:

- If the "author" is one or more known individuals, duration of the Copyright is in part based upon the survival of the individual. For these works, Copyright exists until all the authors die plus 70 years.

- If the "author" is not identified directly, such as in anonymous or work-for-hire situations, Copyright protection has a term of 95 years from publication or 120 years from creation, whichever expires first.

See §302 for reference.

The short answer is Copyright exists for an exceptionally long time.

Now, these durational categories are somewhat fluid, specifically in relation to anonymous authors. Anonymous in this context includes pseudonyms, but generally its means the author is not 'known' when registered.

Should one or more individuals come forward and claim the work as their own, an anonymous work can be attributed. At that time, it is no longer protected for the set time and instead is governed by the life of the author plus 70 years.

This is not very common, as pseudonyms are not as frequently used as they have been historically and attribution - at least through registration - tends to occur.

Still, these are fairly abstract numbers, let's look at an example to get a sense of how long the duration can end up being.

Consider this fictional situation:

One author is twenty and the other is twenty-five. The work is created and registered in 2019. If both authors have a general average life expectancy of about eighty years old -counting from the younger (assuming both die at average life expectancy as stated) that is 60 years from the year of registration to the year of death.

The younger author would die in 2079, after their creative partner. Then the copyright is held by the author's estates for another 70 years, for a total period of 130 years of Copyright protection. Meaning Copyright protection would expire in **2149**.

That is an insanely long time.

And that is just for if someone lived for an expected life expectancy. Say they live longer. Such a long life will extend the duration of Copyright.

It is this duration which makes the registration of works one of the best investments an author, as defined by **Title 17**, can make.

Subsection 1: What Happens When Copyright Expires?

Once the duration of the Copyright has expired, the work is no longer protected by Copyright law. These works are in what is called the public domain - freely available to the public at large for any purpose.

Figuring out if a work is in the public domain can be fairly challenging due to shifting laws and durations. A good rule of thumb is if the work was published prior to 1923, it is available in the public domain. (The year given is for 2019, add one year for every year you are reading this after 2019!)

Article 2: What Rights are Granted

You, as the copyright owner, have six rights that make up full copyright protection. These six rights are:

1. Reproduction;

2. Derivative;

3. Distribution;

4. Public Performance;

5. Display; and

6. Public Performance by Digital Audio Transmission.

These rights are provided in **§106**.

The value of each right does vary with the work being protected. For example, the Display Right may not be as useful for a Literary Work, where as a Sculptural work may be best protected by the same right.

Each Right deserves a full introduction and explanation so you have a clear understanding of what rights and protections you have for your creative works. So, if there are questions questions related to your work in particular that are not covered in this Handbook, please consult an attorney versed in Copyright Law.

Section A: Reproduction Right

The Reproduction Right is the right: "to reproduce the copyrighted work in copies or phonorecords." **§106**.

This Right is sometimes considered the initial right, in terms of the core concept of what a Copyright actually is, because this Right at its core is the right to copy (or commandment for others not to copy) a creative work.

When the taking of a work occurs, it is generally through the copying of the work. Think pirated movies or music as the primary modern examples.

The Reproduction right is the right to permit, limit, grant, or otherwise direct how your work is transformed from the original into multiple copies. This is both copying the creative work in its entirety or only copying part.

A tangible example could be this Handbook. I as the author have the right to prevent people from scanning or duplicating any part or the entirety of this Handbook. I also have the right to give the Reproduction right, in whole or in part, to a publisher to make copies for sale. Or, I personally could make those copies.

Remember, a Copyright work can be in one or more of several categories. Tying Reproduction solely into one category limits the right unnecessarily and a reproduction does not have to keep the same "form."

Consider choreography, the choreographed piece could be for a play, but could be copied exact form into a video, or motion picture. The category of work may or may not have changed, but the Choreographer's right to reproduce the work could be infringed in that manner.

When an author permits copies, it is not necessarily a permanent grant of the right. Instead, it can be temporary. Think of printers, publishers, and film distributors. They are given the right for a period of time, be it a few days or several years. After that term, the Right returns to the author.

For example, the printer could print off hundreds of prints of a drawing on behalf of the author. The printer then returns the original and all copies to the artist, because the printer only had the authority to make the copies and nothing else.

As the first listed right, the Reproduction right is perhaps the most foundational. Each other right is based on a modification of how the original or the copy is enjoyed and communicated to an audience.

Section B: Derivative Works Right

The Derivative right is the right: "to prepare derivative works based upon the copyrighted work."

Like the Reproduction right, a derivative work is a modification of the original. Where a reproduction is a straight copy, a derivative transforms the work somehow.

A derivative work is: "a work based upon one or more preexisting works." **§ 101**.

While this language is sort of vague, there are some specific examples provided in the definition, but more importantly, let's give a couple real world examples.

The Wonderful Wizard of Oz by L. Frank Baum was published in 1900. Metro-Goldwyn-Mayer adapted the story for movies in 1939 with *The Wizard of Oz*. This adaptation is a derivative work where the original work was transformed into a different category of work all together.

Then there is *Don Quixote*, originally released in two parts in 1605 and 1615 by Miguel de Cervantes. By originally published, I mean Miguel de Cervantes sent the manuscript for publication in his native language, Spanish, in those years. It was translated in 1612 and 1620 originally and respectively. Those translations are derivative works as well.

In this context, derivative does not have the same implication of a negative that might come in casual conversation. Where a critic might refer to a work as "derivative," with the implication that the new work lacks creativity, under Copyright such a determination is irrelevant. Derivative at its core, for Copyright, focuses on a <u>transformation or reinterpretation of the original work</u>.

Derivative works are found all the time all over the place. Fan works are derivative works. Movie rights to a graphic novel is a right in a particular kind of derivative. So are toys from the last big blockbuster. Sequels, prequels, and re-imaginings alike are all derivative works. And don't forget covers of songs.

In modern life, authorized or permitted derivative works are big money and can be extremely enjoyable.

Section C: Distribution Right

The Distribution right is the right "to distribute copies or phonorecords of the copyrighted work to the public by sale or other transfer of ownership, or by rental, lease, or lending." **§106**.

This is where retail, theaters, and other points of sale of the work make an impact. Distribution relies on the original creation and the Reproduction right. After all, if there is no work and if there are not enough copies fo the work, it cannot be Distributed to the public.

Consider reading a book. Did you go to you neighborhood big box book retailer and pick it up? Or did you go to the internet and download it for your e-reader? Is there a company that turned it into an audio file and sells it as an audiobook available on demand or on a streaming platform? These are all distribution channels that were granted the right, by the author, to sell it to you in that particular form.

For some works this is the best and most convenient path to reach an audience. The work gets reproduced to a sufficient level and then sent out into the world in a variety of different ways.

However, some works are less easily copied. Consider David by Michelangelo. The sculpture is almost 17 feet tall, carved from marble. It is not really easy or even manageable to copy the original into a comparative or exact work.

Distribution relevance, in this case, is of a derivative, be it photos or miniatures, or extremely limited to the movement of the original. Even if the original is immobile, it doesn't mean the author does not have a distribution right in the work, it just may not be as important a right for the work.

Section D: Public Performance Rights

The Public Performance right is the right: "in the case of literary, musical, dramatic, and choreographic works, pantomimes, and motion pictures and other audiovisual works, to perform the copyrighted work publicly." **§106**.

This public performance right is exactly what it sounds like, even if the definition sounds overly complicated. If you write a play, a poem, or some other work that can be performed, you have the right to permit, or not, a public performance of that creative work.

A great example of this kind of exhibition is a poetry reading. Those authors of poetry standing up on stage are exercising their right to publicly perform their poetry. If the poet has stage fright, they can give the public performance right to a friend.

Another simple example is a play or performance. *The Nutcracker*, attributed to Pyotr Tchaikosky for the score and choreographed by Marius Petipa and Lev Ivanov is a popular event during the holidays. The play was not performed just for family and friends, instead the performance was for large group of unrelated people who showed up to watch the play. It was performed publicly, under this right.

The right of public performance does focus on the "public" side of things too. Keep in mind that if you have a copy of a movie, you have a license to "perform" the movie. I.e. watch it. However, that ability is limited to friends and family in a private gathering. It does not mean you have the right to watch the movie on the side of a two story building with a hundred of your closest friends.

The right to perform it publicly remains with the author.

An important thing to remember is the work does not need to be inherently performative to be protected by this work.

Consider, for example, a novel. There is nothing requiring the novel to be performed, most people read by themselves. Yet, a person can read the work aloud to a group of people and this could be considered a type of public performance.

The Public Performance right and the other rights granted do not have to be fully usable given the work. The right still exists and is still enforceable related to that work.

Section E: Display Rights

The Display right is the right: "in the case of literary, musical, dramatic, and choreographic works, pantomimes, and pictorial, graphic, or sculptural works, including the individual images of a motion picture or other audiovisual work, to display the copyrighted work publicly." **§106.**

Harkening back to David by Michelangelo, people can go see the sculpture in part because of this right.

One way to think of the Display right is it is the right to perform a work publicly, except the work doesn't move. Note this is related to specific categories of works, most obviously in exception to sound recordings. Because of this, the Display right reaches only to the listed works - which is fair because of the final right to be discussed.

The reference to music and choreographic works tends to be read as a reference to how the works are written down - the score and steps. It is the right to display a poster of Beethoven's 5th Symphony, but not to actually play the Symphony.

When thinking of the Display right, some of the best examples are murals and sculptures. These works tend to be bought by a government for the express purpose of having art accessible to the public. There can be an explicit understanding that the work is being commissioned for such purpose of Display.

Another example, though worse, is creative works on display in a museum. As such, a book being presented as a historical piece is being displayed under this right. The reason this is a worse example is most of the time, unless we are discussing museums of modern art, the art and displays in a museum tend to already be in the public domain.

Section F: Public Performance by digital audio transmission

The right of Public Performance by Digital Audio Transmission is: "in the case of sound recordings, to perform the copyrighted work publicly by means of a digital audio transmission." **§106**.

This authorizes the radio and the innovations on that technology, including today's streaming services. Beyond that, check out the public performance section. This right is extremely relevant to music creation and sound recordings.

As this Handbook serves as more of a general introduction, and this is such a specific right, if you are creating a sound recording such as music or a podcast, please consult with a Copyright attorney.

Section G: How to think about these Rights?

These Rights broadly apply to any work, meaning if you create something you have the rights associated with Copyright. Which raises the question, what can you do with a statutory right?

Broadly, there are three options:

1. Nothing,

2. Sell or Rent, and

3. Enforce.

Just because you have a right, does not mean you have to do anything with it, in the context of Copyright. Think of it this way, there are a lot of fan created works, such as stories or art, for different movies and T.V. shows. It is entirely within the copyright owner's power and discretion to enforce all aspects of Copyright in connection with these creators.

Yet, many times, no such action is taken, for any number of reasons.

The reason a Copyright owner can waive a violation of Copyright is fairly simple. There is nothing in **Title 17** requiring enforcement of rights. While there are cases that suggest selective enforcement may be problematic, at the moment, selective enforcement can be the more practical approach to managing this aspect of copyright enforcement.

As for selling or renting the right, those who own the initial Copyright protected work can agree to a License. This is a contract explaining what:

- Rights are being transferred

- Price is being paid

- Time restrictions are included

- Geographic restrictions exist

- And such other provisions and terms as may be appropriate

This is a flexible document, one designed to ensure the author remains constant while the rights holder or owner shifts. Depending on how you want to create, this may be an important document.

Finally, enforcement. This is tied into the concept of infringement. When a bad actor infringes on the rights of the Copyright owner, the owner can enforce the law against that bad actor. More details as to infringement and enforcement are in Article 4.

Article 3: What is this about Registration?

In defining what a copyright is and when it comes into existence, nothing was said about registration. A work is created by an author, it meets the definition, Copyright comes into existence. Take for example the **§106A** rights, which we haven't discussed but are the Moral Rights. They exist for specific works, period. (Again, they are important but are specific not general and will not be covered in this Handbook.) There is no need for governmental input or authority.

That is true. To an extent.

Because Copyright law is Constitutionally created and statutorily defined, the rights of Copyright are enshrined in the Copyright Act. Meaning any and all rights must exist and be triggered in accordance with statutes. There are certain rights that vest automatically, the six described above for example.

However, not all rights are so automatic.

This Article is going to discuss a few reasons to go through with registration and the registration process. Including how registration brings additional rights and protections you may need or want in the future without having to explicitly plan for them.

Section A: Why Register?

As mentioned, when facing a question about Copyright law, it always makes sense to start by looking at the Statutes. It's also important to refer to Article 1 Section D of this Handbook talking about Duration. Recall, a copyright, <u>when registered</u>, has a presumption of time for which it is effective - specifically life of the author plus 70 years or 120 years for anonymous works.

This is one of the most important reasons to consider registering your creative work under Copyright Law.

Shifting to other reasons for registration, the Statutes also declare that: "no civil action for infringement of the copyright in any United States work shall be instituted until preregistration or registration of the copyright claim has been made in accordance with this title." **See §411**.

In other words, you cannot enforce your copyright unless it has been filed with the Library of Congress.

Registration also allow for collection of statutory damages, damages without having to prove the amount of harm. Plus, under certain circumstances a registered copyright can result in the award of attorneys fees. Though some of these awards can be limited based on registration not occurring for more than three months after the first publication. **§412**.

All this generally means that unless a work is registered, you are not able to claim statutory damages or attorney's fees. Meaning the full cost of enforcing your rights is something you must bare.

The opposite is true as well, a valid registration can ease the costs of enforcement.If you win a case establishing copyright infringement, the infringing party may be ordered to pay your attorney fees. **§505**. Along with the mentioned statutory damages.

There are other benefits of registration, tied specifically into the protection of the Copyright. For works protected by Copyright law, there is the ability to provide notice of the copyright - © - along with date of publication and additional information, though no registration is required to use the ©. **§§401-406**. In addition, with a registration, you can petition the Customs Bureau to prevent the importing of infringing works. **§§601-603**.

However, the biggest benefits are in and around litigating the infringement of Copyright. It may not be something you want to pursue, but it is best practice to move for quick registration to take advantage of these abilities. Not only can a registration act as a deterrent for potential bad actors, it can also limit costs later, making it a price worth paying.

The registration fees are limited. The most expensive registration is $400 for a vessel (ocean) design. Most registrations cost around $55. Meaning, for the fee of $55, you can have a registered Copyright that lasts for over a hundred years. For more specific information, visit www.copyright.gov/about/fees/html.

Section B: What is the Registration Process?

There are three parts of registration. For the best results, it helps to complete the first and second parts at the same time. The final part is the action of the Register of Copyrights, within the Library of Congress.

Subsection I: The Application

To register the work, the first step is to file an application with the Library of Congress at copyright.gov. The application covers several specific issues focused on describing the work, who made the work, and other important details. The criteria are listed at **§409** or you can take a look at the forms at https://www.copyright.gov/forms/.

At minimum, the application includes:

- The individual or entity claiming the copyright,

- The authors and their address

- Any agreements as to ownership

- The title of the work

- Publication and creation dates

- Identification of preexisting works if applicable, and

- Any other information requested by the Copyright Office

For this Handbook, we are going to look at two issues in the application, specifically, related to ownership and related to preexisting works.

The party claiming the copyright <u>does not</u> have to be the author of the work. Instead, the application allows for a third party owner to register the copyright. This means the author may or may not be involved with the registration. The focus is on the current, as of the application, ownership of the work.

Think of this as work-for-hire creations. Work-for-hire has the technical meaning of creating under the Copyright act on behalf of another person or organization. This relationship tends to be through patronage or commissions and employment.

Patronage or commissions tend to be important for independent creators. Big media businesses generally have employees or independent contractors creating works for the business.

Regardless of form, each work-for-hire relationship is based on a contract. In the contract there is a provision about ownership of intellectual property. Work-for-hire, generally, means the author owns absolutely nothing of the work and signs a contract agreeing to the fact. There may be attribution in the registration application, but that will depend on the contract and other factors. Keep in mind, work-for-hire is a variation of standard Copyright practice and requires proof of the work-for-hire relationship.

Because of the focus in registration is on ownership, the issue becomes one of ongoing reporting. Should ownership change, after the application, such change of ownership should be filed with the Library of

Congress to ensure proper notice and identification of the correct and current Copyright holder.

Circling back to the concept of patronage or commissions, the patron or person commissioning the work can obtain any number of rights. However, depending on the parties involved, the author frequently retains some or many rights under the Copyright Act.

One example is the art in public places initiatives. A local government commissions an artist to create a sculpture. The sculpture would be possessed by and owned by the local government, but the artist may retain many if not all other rights associated with the copyright.

Depending on the actual language in the contract and the type of work-for-hire, the contract may shift the burden of filing for the copyright along with ownership of the piece.

The other issue is <u>preexisting works</u>. This applies primarily applies to compilations and derivative works, though it can apply to some other types of works as well. If there is no preexisting work, this section may have little to no information in the application.

Let's take the example of a web comic to illustrate a preexisting work. The web comic posts three times a week. Each of those comic pages could be an independent publication and registered independently.

When the author of the web comic compiles the pages into a book for sale online or at a convention, the compilation would need to reference each existing registration. Specifically, the pages previously registered and now included in the compilation.

Alternatively, take a book being adapted into film. The film would be a derivative work and then the application for the film would need to refer to the registration of the book.

There are a couple reasons why these two topics are being covered in the registration section when there is an entire Handbook on Copyright law. The primary reason is each application is reviewed by the Copyright Office. If they compare the work, based on title or content, and find it related to another work as a matter of law, then the registration may be delayed or denied.

Second, sometimes the compilation or derivative is being done by a different party than the author of the original work(s). This is a place where the authority to own and to register the compilation or derivative becomes important. If there is no authority, then problems may arise.

Subsection II: The Deposits

One purpose of the Copyright Office is to ensure the works exist. Not just at the time of registration, but also to create a record for the future, so those who want to know what was registered can get accurate information or enjoyment. In other words, the Library of Congress has been tasked with creating as complete a history of culture as possible. This catalogue and recordation function is encouraged through the registration process.

Note there are fines associated with not providing the samples of the creative work. Though, if you have made a one of a kind sculpture, the sample can be a copy or picture of your work. Or depending on the type of creative work, it may be explicitly exempted from this requirement.

As for timing, the deposit of "two complete copies of the best edition" is to be made within three months of publication of the creative work you are attempting to register. **§407**.

Please note this is not registration! A work can be published before being submitted for registration or a work can be registered prior to publication. There are deposit rules around unpublished works as well, however, the point is you should keep an eye on timing. Send two copies to the Copyright Office within three months of publication.

The Deposit requirement also plays into the examination process. Specifically, if there is no copy of the work available, it can make it difficult to determine if a copyright certificate should be issued. Again this is more for the movable and easily reproduced works. Other types of works have regulations to address and to minimize the complication of submitting a sample.

Subsection III: Examination and Issuance

The application for registration is the start of the process, but the majority of the remainder lies behind the scenes with the Office of Copyright. It is their job to examine and then register the Copyright.

Examination is focused on a couple of key elements.

First, there needs to be confirmation the work: "constitutes copyrightable subject matter." **§410**. Refer back to Article 1 Section B of this Handbook, where we talk about what works can receive Copyright Protection.

Next the Copyright Office has to determine if the application and work comply with: "the other legal and formal requirements of this title." **§410**.

This tends to be answered in the affirmative if there is a complete application and appropriate deposits of the work. If you go through the process carefully, there should be very few issues the majority of the time.

If everything checks out, the copyright is registered and a certificate is sent to you by mail.

If there are issues, a notice of a refusal will be sent instead. Keep in mind this refusal may or may not be final, there are certain circumstances where you can request a reconsideration of the decision.

Upon receipt of the certificate, you are the proud holder of a Copyright with all the rights that confers.

Article 4: Infringement Test

Infringement of a copyright can occur in a variety of ways and times, meaning there are a number of tests which may be used and some appropriate defenses to the accusation.

For this discussion, we will start with who can enforce the copyright, then cover the primary test of infringement, followed by a discussion on Fair Use.

Section A: Enforcement

There are two groups of people able to take action on an infringement of the copyright. The first, and sometimes only, is the "legal or beneficial owner of an exclusive right under copyright." **§501(b)**.

In other words, Copyright law provides a monopoly, a power to prevent others from gaining under your intellectual creations without your approval. The person who is forced to monitor and more importantly to enforce is the owner of the copyright.

It can also include an author who has retained rights or it can be the person or entity to whom the author sold some or all rights. Similar to the application, this is a question of actual ownership, not necessarily of who created the work.

Think, for example, about the adaptation of a book. The author of the book permits the movie studio to adapt the work. That adaptation has it's own copyrights. Meaning if an unscrupulous actor were to infringe, the first question would be was the infringement of the book or the movie. If the infringement was from the book, then the author of the book would have the ability to enforce, where the studio who adapted it may not have the same power.

Think about the consequence of this consideration for you. Depending on the amount of cash on hand, you may not have the resources to take an infringing party to court.

However, the Copyright Act may protect you. One of the benefits of registration is the prevailing party may be awarded attorney fees. Thus, even if you are not equal in size to a media conglomeration, if you have the registration, you have some ability to enforce your rights as the copyright owner.

If you prove infringement there are a number of remedies you can seek. For example, the court can issue an injunction, backed by contempt of court - which can include jail time and a judicial order to the offending party to stop infringing. **§502.**

Alternatively, the infringing works can be impounded by an order of a Judge and destroyed upon request of the author and proof of infringement. **§503.**

Then there are the money damages, which can be anything from the actual damages and lost profits suffered to statutory damages, depending on circumstances. **§504.**

Statutory damages mean any harm done to you can be defined by law. This can be helpful, depending on circumstances. It is an important consideration to note statutory damages are capped in accordance with law. **§504(C)**.

Thus, there are numerous of ways to enforce your copyright. As mentioned, the person who must enforce these rights is the author or owner of the right. This is true, with one exception.

There can be criminal prosecutions against those who are commit "Criminal Infringement" of a copyright by a "person who willfully infringes a copyright." **§506**.

As this is a crime, only governmental prosecutors can bring the case.

The recourse is limited, there are only certain types of infringement that count, such as:

- a minimum dollar value of $1,000,

- pirating,

- and other thefts. **§506(a)(1)**.

Because this is a criminal conviction, the punishments can be anywhere from imprisonment for up to 10 years and or given a fine.

All of this leads to an important question. What should you do if the work you created has been copied or there has been infringement on your rights?

If there is infringement of your work, you have a choice to make:

- What you should pursue in court?

- Is it worth pursuing?

- What remedies should be pursued?

- How strong is your case?

These questions and more need to be discussed with your attorney. Your attorney should be able to help you determine if and to what extent pursuing legal action is justified in your situation.

Section B: Substantially Similar and other tests

When seeking to prove infringement, the test is tied to the facts of the case directly. There is some overarching law, but the majority of infringement cases hinge on a comparison of the original work and the alleged infringing work. As such, until your attorney can sit down and look at the two side by side, the best that can be done is to have a broad understanding of how to prove infringement.

Courts follow the substantial similarity test, in most cases. The courts have said the: "standard test for substantial similarity between two items is whether an 'ordinary observer, unless he set out to detect the disparities, would be disposed to overlook them, and regard [the] aesthetic appeal as the same.'" *Mannion v. Coors Brewing Company*, 377 F. Supp. 2d 444 (S.D.N.Y. 2006) *internal citation omitted.*

This is wonderful legal language.

In other words the test asks two primary questions:

-   "How much" of the original work was copied?

-   Would a neutral observer only see the similarities?

It is important to note there are variations on this test, some with additional factors and others with just different factors. It is always important to consult with an attorney prior to making a determination on infringement.

Sometimes proving infringement is easy. For example, if digital scans of a poster are uploaded to a social media site without approval and infringement likely exists.

Though, even if infringement may be relatively easy to establish, it may be hard to find the actual perpetrator - depending on circumstances.

Other times, infringement is harder to establish and it depends on the type of infringement. After all, if the infringing work is vastly reworked, and more along the lines of taking inspiration rather than copying the original, it can be challenging to prove infringement.

A big issue with the substantial similarity test is that it can be fairly subjective. How different do the two works have to be in order to be seen as unrelated? Is a small change impactful enough to make it unrelated? What if there are big changes that do not change the feel or appearance of the work?

These are questions of not just proof but interpretation and are debated hotly in each case. Yes, there are rules and guidelines, but finding the best application of those rules and guidelines can be a challenge.

Regardless, infringement is a big and complicated area of law, heavily dependent on facts and circumstances, and one that when an issue arises, you need to be consulting an attorney.

Section C: Fair Use and Limitations on Copyright Protection

Copyright law provides a number of protections and rights. However, there is a limit to how far that protection goes. As such, we are going to discuss the most well known defense and mention a couple other limitations.

Fair use of a Copyright protected work can be for: "purposes such as criticism, comment, news reporting, teaching. . ., scholarship, or research." §107.

As such, in writing this Handbook, I could quote from a copyrighted work. A play, a book, a movie, it really wouldn't matter, so long as the use was not to amplify my work by reference but instead to use that work as an educational example. I could use that work and reflect back on it in each section, making it an element of "teaching" or "scholarship."

However, just because the purpose is appropriate for fair use, there are some additional factors to consider. Specifically:

> "(1) the purpose and character of the use, including whether such use is of a commercial nature or is for nonprofit educational purposes;
>
> (2) the nature of the copyrighted work;

(3) the amount and substantiality of the portion used in relation to the copyrighted work as a whole; and

(4) the effect of the use upon the potential market for or value of the copyrighted work." **§107**.

In other words, the question is not just why a person is using the original work, but how much is being used and to what extent does it impact the value of the original work.

Let's take an example. A professor at a university is trying to determine the philosophical ramifications of popular culture through the lens of several schools of thought. In her work, she cites to the superheroes everyone knows. The citations include several full page spreads of several comics. The work is then published as a textbook.

Though the analysis of fair use, the purpose is for academic, scholarship, and teaching purposes. Definitely a positive towards fair use. However, the textbook is being sold, and with textbooks what they are, at a significant commercial price point.

The original work is textual as well as graphic, so there are multiple types of work being infringed. Some superhero works exist for decades with author upon author being hired to expand the world. Which can mean the amount used in a textbook is probably limited, compared to the collection of works as a whole creating the character, and because the superhero is so well known it can be doubtful any textbook impacted the original work significantly.

As such, it is probably fair use given the facts as suggested (reasonable judges will disagree on any case, so **do not** treat this as proof positive your particular use would be protected).

<u>What does this mean? Ultimately, two things.</u>

1. A registered copyright gives an author a lot of power and authority. If they see infringement, they are well within their rights to respond.

2. Those rights and powers are not unlimited. The purpose of Copyright is promote the "arts and sciences." That cannot happen if criticism and other discussions around the work cannot occur.

Fair use is not the only limitation on a Copyright. Many such limitations are for particular rights and particular works.

For example, there is a limitation on the Scope of exclusive rights in sound recordings. **§114**. Another broader right is based in allowing libraries and archives to restore and reproduce certain works. **§108**.

There are others, but the main points are Copyright law protects an original work for an exceptionally long time and enforcement of a Copyright is not unlimited.

Article 5: The Digital Millennium Copyright Act

The internet has changed everything. As the uses for and speed of the internet continues to advance, it continues to change everything.

Social media, streaming services, video on demand, hosted images, and more all are challenges for a copyright holder that did not exist before the internet became accessible to huge swaths of people.

In 1998, Congress acted by passing the Digital Millennium Copyright Act of 1998 (the "DMCA"). Designed to be fairly comprehensive, the DMCA did a lot to change Copyright liability heading into the new digital age.

When a website, or other provider, allows users to upload, store, or transmit data, the website may not know what is or is not infringing material until the website is sued. This puts a lot of risk on platforms with user created content.

This risk lead to the addition of **§512**.

The provision, while sufficiently verbose, provides a safe harbor for service providers. Under **§512**, an author or owner can issue a notice to the website of the existence of infringing material, generally called the takedown notice.

If a website receives the notice, and complies by removing the allegedly infringing material for dispute, the website is not liable for the infringement. However, the takedown notice must be made in good faith and must be accurate to avoid being subject to penalty of perjury.

Is this the best or only way to deal with the issue? Perhaps, perhaps not. But it is a tool for an author or owner to be aware of and to use in the right circumstances.

The other reason this law is raised is to mention something important.

Copyright law is almost constantly in flux. After the Copyright act was enacted in 1976, superseding prior law, the Act has been amended approximately 50 times as of the writing of this Handbook.

In other words, the core rights are and have been well defined. However, the changes in technology, changes in concerns, changes in legal precedent, and changes in the global legal and commercial marketplace all impact the Copyright Act. As such, it is an area which should be monitored regularly by authors and copyright owners.

Article 6: Copyright Checklist

This Handbook has walked through what types of creative works are protectable under Copyright law, general steps to complete registration, benefits of registration and ramification of not following through on registering the Copyright.

This Checklist is designed to cover all of these bases, and help you complete the registration process after a work is created.

☐ Create the work!

☐ Consider the work, if you say yes to the following move forward:

    ☐ Is the work a literary work?

    ☐ Is the work a musical work?

    ☐ Is the work a pantomimes or choreographic work?

- ☐ Is the work a pictorial, graphic, or sculptural work?

- ☐ Is the work a motion picture or other audiovisual work?

- ☐ Is the work a sound recording?

- ☐ Is the work an architectural work?

☐ Create the Deposit works:

- ☐ If published, 2 copies or 2 phonorecords

- ☐ If unpublished, 1 copy or phonorecord

- ☐ Check https://www.copyright.gov/title37/202/37cfr202-19.html for Exemptions from Deposit requirements if deposit copies are challenging.

☐ Apply:

    ☐ Go to https://www.copyright.gov/
registration/ for the application and
complete it

    ☐ Wait to hear . . .

☐ Monitor your Copyright

    ☐ Before and after registration, keep an eye
out for unauthorized copies, theft, or other
uses of you work.

    ☐ If such use occurs, decide how to proceed
with your lawyer.

☐ Create more Copyrightable works!

About the Author

Brian Hanning is the founder and sole attorney for Hanning Law Limited. He earned a bachelors degree from Colorado State University's College of Business and a juris doctor degree from Michigan State University College of Law. Combining these interests and skill sets sent him on the path towards owning his own firm to connect with and support clients in a more personal and impactful way. Brian is a member of the Colorado Bar and assists entrepreneurs, small businesses, and creative industry clients primarily in the Northern Colorado area.

Brian practices transactional law with a focus on helping small business owners understand what laws can apply to their businesses, and the risks and benefits associated with certain decisions. He also volunteers with Colorado Attorneys for the Arts to share his expertise and hands on client experience with artists around the State.

Outside of work, Brian spends a lot of time with family -most importantly the three family dogs. He enjoys living and working in Fort Collins, Colorado with an abundance of delicious and interesting local coffee shops and microbreweries. Brian ends up at both establishments frequently, meeting with all sorts of amazing people.